4/02

AIRCRAFT

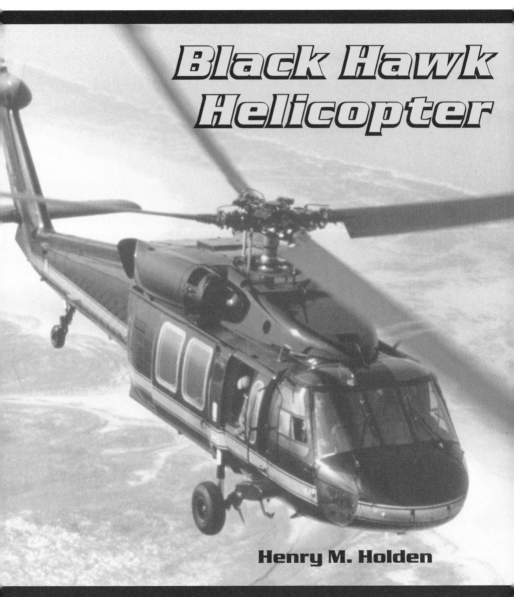

Black Hawk Helicopter

Henry M. Holden

Enslow Publishers, Inc.

40 Industrial Road   PO Box 38
Box 398   Aldershot
Berkeley Heights, NJ 07922   Hants GU12 6BP
USA   UK

http://www.enslow.com

To my grandson, Cameron, with love.

Library of Congress Cataloging-in-Publication Data

Holden, Henry M.
    Black Hawk helicopter / Henry M. Holden.
        p. cm. — (Aircraft)
    Includes bibliographical references (p.   ) and index.
    ISBN 0-7660-1568-8
        1. Black Hawk (Military transport helicopter)—Juvenile literature.
    2. Aeronautics, Military—United States—Juvenile literature. 3. Helicopters
    in search and rescue operations—Juvenile literature. [1. Black Hawk
    (Military transport helicopter) 2. Aeronautics, Military. 3. Helicopters.]
    I. Title. II. Aircraft (Berkeley Heights, N.J.)
    UG1232.T72 .H65 2001
    623.7'465—dc21
                                                            00-010745

Printed in the United States of America

10 9 8 7 6 5 4 3 2 1

To Our Readers: All Internet Addresses in this book were active and appropriate
when we went to press. Any comments or suggestions can be sent by e-mail to
Comments@enslow.com or to the address on the back cover.

Photo Credits: © Corel Corporation, pp. 13, 21, 26, 34, 37; David Creech,
pp. 35, 39; Department of Defense photo by Spike Call, U.S. Navy, p. 14;
Henry M. Holden, pp. 10, 19, 22, 27, 29, 31, 32; Larry Karson, p. 7; Sikorsky
Helicopters/United Technologies, Inc., pp. 16, 40, 42; U.S. Coast Guard, p. 23;
U.S. Customs Service, pp. 4–5, 8, 11, 12, 18.

Cover Photo: U.S. Customs Service

Contents

CHAPTER 1

Pursuing
Drug Smugglers

UH-60 Black Hawk Helicopter

It is October 31, 1987—Halloween night—in Miami, Florida. The weather could hardly be worse at Homestead Air Force Base. Fierce winds push heavy clouds, and blasts of lightning rip the air. A thunderclap shakes the U.S. Customs Aviation Branch building.

At the base, U.S. Customs pilots of the Miami Aviation Branch wait, knowing that a night of bad weather is a good night for aerial drug smugglers. The pilots' job is to nab people flying illegal drugs into the country.

In anticipation of a busy night, Tim Riordan puts on his flight suit and straps on his pistol. Riordan is one of the two Black Hawk helicopter pilots on alert duty. There are also two Citationjet pilots on alert. He heads for the Customs ready room where the other pilots are waiting.

Supervisor Larry Karson is monitoring the radio, writing everything down. "FAA radar is reporting an unidentified aircraft inbound from the east. Probably coming in from the Bahamas. No flight plan. Let's go catch them," he says, hitting the alarm button to alert the pilots in the ready room.[1]

Riordan and his copilot head for the Black Hawk. The pilots will attempt to catch the suspected drug smugglers. Another team jogs to a Cessna Citationjet sitting on the rain-soaked ramp. Four U.S. Customs air officers, called the Bust Team, follow Riordan silently to the Black Hawk helicopter. They are all wearing bulletproof vests and are armed with pistols, automatic rifles, and handcuffs. Their job, once they are back on the ground, will be to act as police officers and arrest the suspects.

The Black Hawk helicopter is a $6-million machine equipped with the latest in high-tech wonders. The U.S. Customs Service uses it like a police department uses a cruiser: to chase suspected drug smugglers. It can fly at

Larry Karson stands next to *CokeBuster*, a U.S. Customs Black Hawk helicopter. The white snowflakes and green leaves on the side of the helicopter show how many drug airplanes have been captured with this aircraft.

over 200 miles per hour and can stay in the air for almost five hours.[2]

Minutes later, the Black Hawk lifts into the darkness. The Citationjet is not far behind. It overtakes the Black Hawk and, with its forward-looking infrared sensor (FLIR), becomes the eyes of the Black Hawk team.

The FLIR can find other aircraft during the day or night. It can detect the heat from an aircraft's body and engine and display it on a monitor similar to a television screen.

A Black Hawk helicopter followed by two Cessna Citationjets fly over the Houston Astrodome. Citationjets fly with the Black Hawk when chasing drug-smuggling planes.

≡ The Chase Is On

The four officers on the Black Hawk are buckled in with seatbelts and shoulder harnesses. They can listen to each other and to the copilot and pilot by using headsets— helmets with a microphone and speakers. It is impossible to hear without them because of the noise from the engines and rotors. The rotors are the blades on the top and the tail of the helicopter. Radio communication between the base, the Citationjet, and the Black Hawk is constant. The pilot and copilot on the Black Hawk wear night-vision goggles.

"Target at two o'clock and three miles," says the FLIR operator in the Citationjet.

"I don't see him," replies Riordan.

"He's flying without lights," responds the FLIR operator.

The officers in the back of the Black Hawk strain to see the target in the darkness, but it is impossible.

"Target one mile, still at two o'clock," the FLIR operator reports.

The wind is pushing the helicopter all over the sky. The Black Hawk banks left, then right.

"I see him!" Riordan exclaims as a pale green image of the airplane appears in his night-vision goggles. "He's going in, and I'm on him." He puts the helicopter into a rapid descent.

The crew can no longer see Homestead Air Force Base, far behind them. Blackness surrounds the helicopter. The smugglers should have no idea they are being followed, because the Black Hawk is flying without lights. Riordan relies on his instruments to fly safely.

The suspected smugglers' airplane flicks on its landing lights. It is only a few feet over an open field. It lands quickly and rolls to a stop.

"Check your gear, and don't forget to take off your headsets," the lead air officer on the Black Hawk says over the radio to his Bust Team.[3]

Riordan hovers just two feet off the ground, in front of the smugglers' airplane. The copilot flips on the powerful Nightsun searchlight, beaming it on the smugglers' aircraft. The Nightsun searchlight is as bright as 30 million candles, and the scene appears to be in daylight. The Black

The forward-looking infrared sensor (FLIR) is mounted under the nose of the Black Hawk. The Nightsun, mounted next to the left wheel of the Black Hawk, is as bright as 30 million candles.

Hawk comes in so fast that the two men in the airplane freeze, like deer caught in headlights. The Bust Team jumps out, guns drawn, to surround and arrest the suspects. A third suspect, in an off-road vehicle, starts his engine and hightails it down a road alongside an orange grove.

In moments, the Bust Team has the men from the airplane in custody. The Black Hawk begins to chase the escaping man in the off-road vehicle. The copilot lights up the driver with the searchlight, but that does not stop him. He is fleeing for his life. If he is caught, he could spend ten years in federal prison.

The U.S. Customs Service officers cover the crew of a suspected smuggler airplane. The Black Hawk helicopter gets in front of the small airplane to prevent him from taking off.

Riordan runs the helicopter even with the suspect. The Black Hawk's main rotor blade nearly clips the tops of the trees. One wrong move and the chopper will crash and burn.

The suspect jams on the brakes and spins the vehicle around to face the oncoming helicopter. He is reversing direction in an attempt to escape the helicopter.

Riordan is worried. If the smuggler starts shooting and hits the tail rotor, the chopper could crash. There is only one thing to do.

Riordan moves the helicopter so that the Nightsun is shining on the vehicle and blinding the driver. The driver

This suspect is now in custody. The U.S. Customs air officers handcuff him.

is distracted by the helicopter, its noise, and the powerful downdraft of the rotor blades. Blinded by the searchlight, he does not see the danger ahead. The vehicle runs off the road and into a ditch. The driver is thrown forward into the windshield. The Citationjet circles overhead, watching the action on its FLIR. "The suspect is lying on the ground next to his vehicle," the FLIR operator reports. "He is not moving."

A few minutes later the Bust Team reports that they have the third suspect in custody. He has a scalp wound from impacting his windshield. He and the other men were smuggling cocaine. They will spend a long time in jail.

CHAPTER 2

Special Equipment and Missions

The Sikorsky Black Hawk helicopter is one of the most advanced helicopters in the world. It serves in many different missions. As a military helicopter the Black Hawk can carry up to thirteen combat-equipped troops, or soldiers, in most weather conditions.[1] American troops fight in battle and guard places like Bosnia, Kosovo, and Haiti.

The U.S. Army and the Marine Corps also use the Black Hawk as a gunship. It can be armed with machine guns or cannons on special external brackets. The Black Hawk is also a tank killer. It can carry sixteen laser-guided, armor-piercing missiles or 10,000 pounds of rockets and missiles.

The U.S. Navy calls their version of the Black Hawk the Seahawk. It is used to carry supplies between Navy ships and to launch missiles against enemy ships. The Seahawk can also drop mines and make smokescreens to cover ships from enemy fire. The U.S. Coast Guard calls the Black Hawk the Jayhawk and uses it for search and rescue.

The U.S. Air Force uses the Black Hawk for Special Operations and special electronic missions in which it jams enemy communications. They call it the Pave Hawk.

In civilian (non-military) mode, the Black Hawk is used to fly injured people to hospitals. It also flies police officers to crime scenes and chases suspects. The Black Hawk is

A missile roars off a U.S. Navy SH-60 Seahawk helicopter toward a laser designated surface target.

important during other emergencies, too. In the United States, it is used to evacuate people after hurricanes and to rescue flood victims when the roads are unusable. It delivers supplies such as food, water, and medicine to help the victims. It is also used to fight forest fires. The National Aeronautics and Space Administration (NASA) uses one for in-flight research.

Instruments and Controls

The Black Hawk helicopter is 64 feet, 10 inches long—about the length of two school buses. Instead of having wings like an airplane, it has one main rotor, 53 feet in diameter, attached to the top of it. The main rotor has four blades that whirl around. The air rushes over and under the blades, which lifts the helicopter—much as it would lift an airplane's wings. The word *helicopter* comes from two Greek words: *heliko*, which means "spiral" or "turn" and *pteron*, which means "wing." So, the word *helicopter* actually means "turning wings."

All helicopters have the same basic flight instruments. The altimeter shows how high the helicopter is flying. The airspeed indicator works like a speedometer and displays the vehicle's speed through the air. Engine gauges tell the pilot whether the engine is running hot or cold and whether it has enough oil pressure. The Black Hawk has all these flight instruments and a few special ones.

The fast, large, flexible Black Hawk has high-quality flight controls that allow the helicopter to move in quick,

The Firehawk is a civilian version of the Black Hawk. It can carry up to 15 firefighters to a fire zone or drop 1,000 gallons of water on a forest fire. Its water tank is attached to the bottom of the helicopter. Its snorkel-like water pump can pump 1,000 gallons from a lake in one minute.

coordinated movements to avoid being hit by bullets and missiles. If it is struck by gunfire, this amazing helicopter may switch to its backup electrical and hydraulic systems. The hydraulic systems use pressurized liquids, such as oil, to make the helicopter easier to fly. Its fuel tanks are self-sealing, which means that in a crash landing, there is less chance of an explosion due to a fuel leak. The landing gear and crew seats are designed to absorb energy, which means that hard or violent landings will not necessarily injure the crew. The seats and side panels in the cockpit are also bulletproof.

Power and Speed

Because it carries so much equipment, the Black Hawk weighs almost 22,000 pounds. That is more than 11 tons. Its two engines combined have almost 4,000 horsepower. (A car has about 150 to 200 horsepower.)

Some helicopters burn gasoline. However, the Black Hawk helicopter burns high-grade kerosene, also known as jet fuel, in its turbine engines.

The Black Hawk helicopter can fly at more than 200 miles per hour. It can climb almost 3,000 feet per minute. Nevertheless, the pilot has rules to follow. The pilot has to fly a specific flight plan, which is like an invisible highway in the sky, and has to continuously tell the air traffic controller where the chopper is and where it is going.

Some Black Hawk helicopters have an autopilot. This automatic system is similar to cruise control in an automobile, but it also provides steering. It makes the

The forward-looking infrared sensor (FLIR) can detect the heat coming from an airplane or tank's engine, and shows it on a monitor.

helicopter easier to fly and helps the pilot stay on course. The autopilot takes the strain out of flying at night and in bad weather.

Some Black Hawk helicopters have an onboard flight computer. The flight computer, an important part of the Black Hawk, does not look like a home computer. It is a panel of switches and gauges that monitors the functions of the helicopter such as engine temperature and fuel flow to the engines. The flight computer makes the helicopter safer to fly. It helps the pilots by monitoring some of the flight systems so that they can concentrate on flying the helicopter.

The panels and switches on the flight computer of the Black Hawk monitor the functions of the helicopter.

☰ *First Test Under Fire*

Troops of the 82nd Airborne Division of the U.S. Army were among the first to fly Black Hawk helicopters on combat missions. This was in Operation Urgent Fury, in Grenada, in October 1983. "On Sunday, October 23, the United States received an urgent formal request . . . to assist in a joint effort to restore order and democracy on the island of Grenada," said President Ronald Reagan.[2]

On the morning of October 26, 1983, several thousand U.S. Army Air Cavalry and Marines landed on the island of Grenada. President Reagan had learned that nearly 1,000 American civilians and medical students were in danger of being held captive by a brutal gang who had violently seized the government.[3] The army and marines evacuated the American civilians and placed U.S. Army Rangers at important locations to block the enemy's advance. The Black Hawk helicopter was an important tool in restoring peace to the island.

Operation Urgent Fury was the Black Hawk's first test under fire, and it proved it could take a lot of punishment. One pilot kept flying the Black Hawk despite seventy-six bullet holes in its fuselage, or body. Another Black Hawk took forty-seven hits, including some in the cockpit, and still landed safely.[4]

In 1991 the Black Hawk flew combat in the Persian Gulf War during Operation Desert Storm. The Black Hawk transported supplies from ships to desert bases in Saudi Arabia, carried wounded to hospitals, and flew Special Operations troops into enemy territory for secret missions.

Jayhawk to the Rescue

When the Coast Guard is called to search for and rescue people on lakes, rivers, and the ocean, and even in the mountains of Alaska, they sometimes use the Jayhawk. It is the largest helicopter in their fleet. It carries a four-person crew: two pilots, a flight mechanic, and a rescue swimmer.[5] Its flight computer can be programmed to fly the helicopter. This means that it can land or take off without the pilot holding the controls. The Coast Guard uses the flight computer when the crew cannot see the water below. It can also use the flight computer as an

The Black Hawk serves as a military helicopter. It can carry Special Operations troops into enemy territory.

Lieutenant Commander Stephen Torpey (left) and Lieutenant Jeffrey McCullars are U.S. Coast Guard Jayhawk pilots.

autopilot, setting a course for the helicopter to fly, so that the pilots can look out the windows to search for people.

When a Mayday call from a disabled boat comes over the radio, everyone at the nearest Coast Guard station swings into action. The Coast Guard launches a search-and-rescue mission, or SAR. "When we get a Mayday call that a boat is in trouble, we have to move fast," said Lieutenant Jeffrey McCullars, a Jayhawk pilot. "We know that lives depend on how fast we get to the scene. We can take off in just a few minutes."[6]

The pilots will have an idea of the boat's location from the radio transmission, so they program it into a computer.

During an ocean rescue, the Jayhawk lifts the U.S. Coast Guard rescue swimmer from the sea.

Based on the tides and winds at the boat's location, the computer tells the pilot where the boat may have drifted. The pilots then program this information into the flight computer on the helicopter.

"We also have a Global Positioning Satellite [GPS] system that will help guide us to within a few feet of the boat," said McCullars. "Then we head out to rescue the people on the boat."

During a SAR, the Jayhawk can fly very slowly so that the pilots have a chance to look for a small boat in the big ocean. If it flies fast, the waves rush by so quickly, it is hard to spot a small boat or people in the water. With its additional external fuel tanks, the Jayhawk can travel about 700 miles—instead of 550 miles—before it needs refueling.

During bad weather or darkness, the Coast Guard uses the forward-looking infrared sensor (FLIR) on the Jayhawk to find boats that are sinking or whose engines are not working.

"Even if it is raining, we can see the ocean on our FLIR screen," said McCullars. "The flight computer can fly us right down to the wave tops, just a few feet off the ocean, so the rescue swimmer can jump into the water. We don't have to touch the controls, and the computer flies into a nice stable hover."[7]

If there are people stranded in the water, the rescue swimmer jumps into the water from the Jayhawk and helps each person. One by one, the people are lifted aboard the Jayhawk in a basket attached to a rescue hoist. The rescue swimmer can swim for a long time. He is the last one to be lifted back aboard the Jayhawk. The pilots then fly the people to a nearby hospital to check for injuries.

The Black Hawk is exciting to fly. The pilots must be highly skilled: it takes many hours of classroom work and training to become a Black Hawk pilot.

Specifications for

Black Hawk Helicopter Model 60L

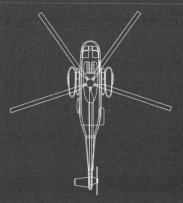

Manufacturer—Sikorsky Helicopters/United Technologies, Inc.

Length—64 feet 10 inches

Height—16 feet 10 inches

Main rotor diameter—53 feet

Fuel—Jet fuel (high-grade kerosene), up to 740 gallons

Maximum speed—207 miles per hour

Cruising speed—150 miles per hour

Rate of vertical climb—2,750 feet per minute

Maximum altitude—about 16,000 feet

Service altitude (the altitude to fly the aircraft for best performance)—about 9,150 feet

Maximum hover altitude—about 11,125 feet

Maximum number of passengers—13

Crew—two pilots, one mechanic, sometimes a fourth such as a rescue swimmer or machine gunner

Endurance (the time it can stay in the air)—about 5 hours

Distance on internal fuel tanks—about 550 miles; optional external tanks can add 150 miles

Engines—Two T700-GE-701C Turboshaft; 1,940 horsepower each

Empty weight—11,516 pounds

Gross weight (maximum weight with fuel and personnel on board)—about 22,000 pounds

Cargo hook capacity—8,000–9,000 pounds

Rescue hoist capacity—600 pounds

CHAPTER 3

Flying the Black Hawk

ach time a pilot goes to fly the Black Hawk, he or she must complete a preflight checklist. This checklist outlines a visual inspection of the helicopter. The pilot looks for cracks or damage on the helicopter and checks the oil in the engines, transmissions, and hydraulic systems. He or she inspects the blades of the main rotor and tail rotor and makes sure the tires on the landing gear are properly inflated and not worn. There are approximately ninety-one items on the preflight checklist.

After the preflight is completed, the pilot can start the engines. On the Black Hawk, there is one Start button for each engine. The buttons are located on the power control levers overhead, between the pilot and the copilot.

"The power control levers are like the gas pedal in a car and send fuel to the engines. There is an Off position, an Idle position, and a Fly position. Once both engines are at Idle and warmed up, the pilot pushes the power control levers to the Fly position," David Creech, a U.S. Army Black Hawk pilot, explained.[1]

The individual controls on the Black Hawk are not difficult to understand. However, the relationship between

Before flying the Black Hawk, a pilot must check many things, including the engines. The powerful engines on the Black Hawk can lift 9,000 pounds. Here it is lifting an Army vehicle.

the controls makes the Black Hawk helicopter more challenging to fly than an airplane. "The basic difference between flying an airplane and the Black Hawk is during landing," said Lieutenant Jeffrey McCullars. "Most fixed-wing pilots will be able to fly a helicopter; however, when landing and in a hover, each of the three main controls require simultaneous adjustments."[2]

≡ Understanding the Controls

There are three main controls on the Black Hawk, and the pilot uses both hands, both feet, and the fingers to adjust them. The cyclic pitch control is mounted on the floor between the pilot's knees. With the right hand, the pilot pushes this control forward to fly straight ahead and pulls it back to fly backward. Pushing it left or right will make the helicopter go sideways. By putting the cyclic pitch control exactly in the center and holding it very still, the pilot can make the helicopter hover.

By pressing a button on the cyclic called the trigger switch, the pilot can talk on the radio to the control tower or to the other people on board the helicopter. Another button on the cyclic is the trim switch. The pilot can move it up, down, left, or right to make small adjustments in the direction of the helicopter.

The second control is the collective pitch control. This lever is on the floor on the left side of the pilot. Pulling up on this lever makes the helicopter go up. Pushing it down makes the helicopter go down. When raised or lowered, this control increases or decreases the angle of all the

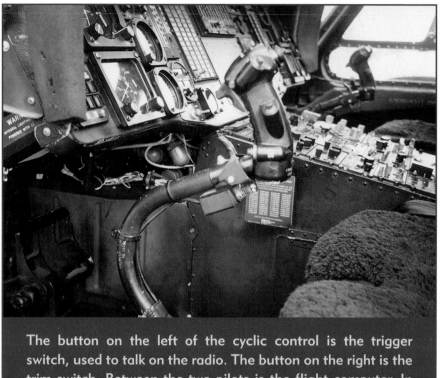

The button on the left of the cyclic control is the trigger switch, used to talk on the radio. The button on the right is the trim switch. Between the two pilots is the flight computer. In the lower left are the tail rotor pedals.

rotor blades collectively. This in turn increases or decreases the amount of lift that the rotor produces.

The third control is the tail rotor pedals, which are mounted on the floor. Pushing the left pedal forward brings the right pedal back and turns the helicopter to the left. Pushing the right pedal forward brings the left pedal back and turns the helicopter to the right.

The Black Hawk is more complicated to fly than other helicopters. People need high levels of training to fly the helicopter and operate the equipment.

"You need to know math, science, English, and play team sports," said McCullars. "Flying this helicopter involves teamwork. You also need good verbal communication skills so that everyone understands what the other person is saying."[3]

The First Step

To fly a Black Hawk helicopter in the U.S. Army, pilots first have to become pilots of simpler, single-engine helicopters. They accomplish this during an eight-month basic flight course. Once they become U.S. Army or Coast Guard pilots, some are chosen to continue with Black Hawk training.

There is a strict selection process for this advanced training. For example, the Coast Guard may need only three Jayhawk pilots from the next class of forty flight students. The students with the best flight tests and academic grades are chosen.[4]

Advanced Training

Pilots selected for Black Hawk training go to a six-week course at Fort Rucker, Alabama. Since the Black Hawk student has already graduated from flight school, the Black Hawk training is an adjustment from one aircraft to another. During the course, students learn how to fly the multiengined Black Hawk and to read more flight instruments. They also attend classes about the Black Hawk's systems. They study the engines and power trains; fuel systems; start, shutdown, and emergency procedures; and the aerodynamics of the Black Hawk. They also learn how to use night-vision goggles.[5]

Advanced training is needed to fly the Jayhawk, pictured here. It has FLIR, a Global Positioning Satellite system, and moving map software, all in the bubble in the nose. On each side is an extra 120-gallon fuel tank.

Night-vision goggles look like alien eyeglasses. They help the pilot to see at night—a boost to the FLIR. With the FLIR seeing heat differences, the goggles intensify the light from the moon, stars, and the ground 2,000 to 3,500 times. Even on the darkest night there is enough light in the sky to allow pilots using night-vision goggles to see.[6]

The pilot does not see as if it were daylight, however. He or she sees everything in pale green. Night-vision goggles are small and portable and can fit on a flight helmet. Students first learn how to use these goggles through interactive computer-based training that uses

This flight helmet has night-vision goggles, which allows the pilot to see in the dark. The pilot's flight helmet also has a built-in microphone and radio earphones so he can communicate with people in the helicopter and on the ground.

sound, video, graphics, and animation to simulate real-life situations.

About four of the six weeks of Black Hawk training are spent in a flight simulator.[7] Simulators are a safe yet realistic way to train pilots in the many steps necessary to fly a Black Hawk. The Black Hawk simulator is like a video game. The inside looks like the inside of the helicopter with all the flight controls. The pilot "flies" the helicopter on a large screen, the kind found in the arcade game Steel Talons, which features a Black Hawk helicopter. The simulator can throw many problems at the student to test his or her level of knowledge. It gives the student important practice in how to react to malfunctioning systems and in-flight emergencies. If the student makes a mistake, he or she does not damage the helicopter—or get hurt. The instructor will ask the students many questions to make sure they understand what they have learned. When a student becomes efficient at flying the helicopter in the simulator and has learned all the lessons in the classroom, he or she will begin actual flight training in the Black Hawk helicopter.

During the training course, students focus on basic tasks such as hovering, ground taxiing, taking off, and following traffic patterns and landing approaches. They practice emergency procedures. Students take flights during the day and at night. They practice using night-vision goggles on board the Black Hawk during an actual night flight. The pilots also learn how to fly special maneuvers so that they can safely fly over a battlefield without getting shot down.

There are many assignments a Black Hawk pilot may receive after training. One assignment that an army pilot may receive is flying a medevac helicopter.

CHAPTER 4

The Medevac Mission

t is June 23, 1999. It is quiet at Camp Able Sentry, the base for the 159th Medical Company, in Skopje, Macedonia. Suddenly, a call comes in.[1] U.S. Marines have been fired upon. At least one person has been killed, and two others have been wounded.[2] The wounded men need to be taken to a hospital. The alarm goes off, and the medevac helicopter crew races to the Black Hawk.

"Tower, this is Dustoff Forty-four requesting permission to take off."

"Dustoff Forty-four, cleared for takeoff," the tower replies.

When the Black Hawk helicopter flies a medevac—or *medical evacuation*—mission, the pilots use call signs so that the control tower will know one helicopter from another. *Dustoff* is a call sign that stands for "*dedicated unhesitating support to our fighting forces.*"

Dustoff pilots are trained to take off in five to eight minutes so that they can pick up injured and wounded soldiers. They do this by having their helicopters on standby. They start the engines at the beginning of the day to make sure they are working properly. The pilots call this a run-up. The crew also has all of their medical

The medevac Black Hawk may have to fly wounded soldiers to a ship's hospital for more treatment. Here, a Black Hawk medevac is about to land on an aircraft carrier. The pods on the sides are external fuel tanks that each carry 250 gallons of fuel.

equipment in place in the helicopter. When they get the call, all they have to do is board the helicopter, go over the preflight checklist, and restart the engines.

≡ The Crew in Control

The Black Hawk medevac carries a crew of four people. The pilot and copilot fly the helicopter. A crew chief makes sure there are no mechanical problems. The flight medic treats the wounded soldiers and stabilizes them as they are being flown to the hospital.

When a Dustoff flight takes off, the crew knows that a wounded soldier must receive expert care within the golden hour. The golden hour is the first sixty minutes after the soldier is wounded, when his life is in the most danger. If he arrives at the hospital within this hour, he has the best chance of surviving his wounds.

When the medevac lands at the battle site, the flight medic and the crew chief supervise the loading of the wounded. They are connected to the cockpit through an intercom. They do not unplug from the intercom in case they receive incoming enemy fire and have to take off quickly. If they have to help load the wounded, extra-long microphone cords allow them some freedom of movement outside the aircraft.

As Dustoff 44 approaches the landing zone (LZ), U.S. Marines at the LZ wait for the chopper to settle on the ground. Then two marines carry each wounded man on a stretcher. Another marine runs alongside each stretcher holding up an intravenous bottle, feeding fluid into the

The Black Hawk's engines kick up dust as the medevac approaches landing.

wounded man. All three scrunch down beneath the broad spinning blades that swirl only a few feet over their heads. The pilot does not shut down the engines because the helicopter will have to take off in a matter of seconds.

The LZ is noisy and dirty. The chopper's engines continue their high-pitched whine, a sharp contrast to the solid *whup, whup, whup* of the blades. The downdraft from the rotor blades kicks up clouds of dust, dirt, and grass that swirl around the marines. They duck their heads and try to cover their faces from the dust. They push through the small dust storm and continue toward the flight medic, who is standing in the doorway of the helicopter. The pilot and copilot watch the loading of the wounded and continue to scan the area. They are worried about incoming enemy fire while they are on the ground. This is a dangerous time for a helicopter crew.

After the wounded are on board the medevac, the flight medic tends to their wounds and the helicopter takes off. Seldom do more than fifteen or twenty seconds pass between the time the helicopter lands and the crew in back reports they are ready to take off.

The pilot says, "Engine power control levers are at fly, systems are all in the green, avionics are as required. Crew, passengers, and mission equipment check. Is everyone secured?"

The copilot says, "Secured front right."

"Secured left rear," the medic reports.

"Secured right," reports the crew chief.

The safety of the marines on the ground is important, and the crew has to make sure the ground personnel are clear of the aircraft before it takes off.

The pilot then asks, "Cleared left, right, and above?"

The medic replies, "Clear up on the left."

"Clear right," calls the crew chief, seeing that no people are near the tail rotor of the rising helicopter.

"Coming up," calls the pilot as he lifts off.[3]

And off they go. En route to the hospital, the flight medic will be busy treating the wounded men.

When Dustoff 44 takes off with patients on board, its call sign changes. It becomes Evac 44. The pilot may say, "Tower, this is Evac Forty-four on a one-mile final. We have two injured on board. Do you copy?" This tells the

When the Landing Zone is too small for landing, the Black Hawk can lower a sling on its rescue hoist and pick up a wounded person.

control tower that the medevac helicopter is one mile from the field and is bringing in two wounded.

The tower replies, "Evac Forty-four, copy loud and clear. You are cleared for a straight-in approach." With injured on board, the tower will let the pilot come in ahead of all the other helicopters and airplanes, including passenger-carrying transport aircraft. When it lands, nurses and a doctor meet the helicopter.

Using helicopters to fly wounded soldiers to hospitals started during the Korean War in 1950. In Korea, helicopters were used to evacuate wounded soldiers in large numbers. In those days they flew the wounded to

This civilian medevac carries external fuel tanks and some of the same equipment found on the Army version of the helicopter. It is used on rescue missions.

field hospitals called Mobile Army Surgical Hospitals, or M.A.S.H units. Today these field hospitals are called Combat Surgical Hospitals (CSH). The pilots call them CASH.[4]

≡ *Inside the Medevac Helicopter*

The Black Hawk medevac helicopter is like a hovering hospital, ambulance, and emergency room all in one. It has a state-of-the-art interior crammed with $1.5 million worth of medical equipment. It can carry up to six seriously wounded soldiers on motorized stretchers that can move up and down.

The onboard medical equipment includes oxygen-generating equipment, respirators, heart monitors, intravenous bottles, and suction devices for cleaning wounds. The Black Hawk also has an infrared camera that can help find the wounded at night. If the helicopter cannot get into the landing zone because of high trees, an external electrical rescue hoist is used to lift soldiers off the ground. The rescue hoist can lift up to 600 pounds. A cargo hook can lift up to about 8,000 pounds, so it can be used to lift heavy equipment such as a jeep or a small truck.[5]

The medevac helicopter saves valuable time that, for some injured soldiers, may make the difference between life and death.

Today the Black Hawk helicopter flies many different missions. It chases airborne drug smugglers, flies soldiers into battle, and transports wounded to hospitals. It serves to fight forest fires and rescues people from the ocean. It can carry high-tech equipment that can "see" in the dark, or it can carry medical equipment found in hospital emergency rooms. It is used for secret missions, and it can fire missiles. The Black Hawk is an impressive aircraft.

Black Hawk Helicopter Models[6]

S-70 Firehawk

EH-60A/L—A special warfare helicopter that carries electronic equipment to intercept and jam enemy communications.

HH-60J Jayhawk—Used by the U.S. Coast Guard to search for and rescue people stranded in the ocean or other remote areas.

MH-60G/L Pave Hawk —With missiles or other weapons on both sides of the fuselage, it is used for attack missions or to sneak in and remove Special Operations troops.

MH-60K Special Operations Aircraft—Flies troops into enemy territory for secret missions.

S-70 Firehawk—Used to fight large forest fires.

SH-60B/S-70B Seahawk—Used by the U.S. Navy for antiship and antisubmarine surveillance.

UH-60A—A light transport helicopter used for air assault and medevac units.

UH-60Q Medevac—Flies medical evacuation missions.

VH-60—An executive transport helicopter sometimes used by the President.

YEH-60B—Special version of the Black Hawk that detects moving targets on the battlefield and downlinks the information to an army ground station.

SH-60B Seahawk

MH-60L Pave Hawk

HH-60J Jayhawk

Chapter Notes

Chapter 1. Pursuing Drug Smugglers

1. Author interview with Larry Karson, former Miami Air Branch Supervisor, December 9, 1998.

2. *U.S. Customs Air Interdiction, A Primer* (Washington, D.C.: U.S. Customs Service, Office of Aviation Operations).

3. Actual conversation on October 31, 1987, over South Florida, as related to author by Larry Karson, December 9, 1998.

Chapter 2. Special Equipment and Missions

1. *Jane's Encyclopedia of Aviation* (New York: Portland House, 1989), p. 815.

2. "Text of Reagan's Announcement of the Invasion of Grenada," *The New York Times*, October 26, 1983, p. A16.

3. Ibid.

4. Sikorsky Aircraft Corporation, <http://www.sikorsky.com/programs/blackhawk/inaction.html> (April 27, 2000).

5. *All About Helicopters*, video (Truckee, Calif.: Bill Aaron Productions, 1995).

6. Author correspondence with Lieutenant Jeffrey McCullars, Jayhawk pilot, February 7, 2000.

7. Author interview with Lieutenant Jeffrey McCullars, Jayhawk pilot, July 30, 1999.

Chapter 3. Flying the Black Hawk

1. Author correspondence with Chief Warrant Officer David Creech, Army Black Hawk pilot, September 5, 1999.

2. Author correspondence with Lieutenant Jeffrey McCullars, Jayhawk pilot, February 7, 2000.

3. McCullars, July 30, 1999.

4. McCullars, February 7, 2000.

5. Author correspondence with Chief Warrant Officer David Sheppard, Army Black Hawk pilot, July 19, 1999.

6. U.S. Army, *Night Flight Techniques and Procedures*, publication number TCI-204, December 1988, pp. 2–7.

7. Sheppard.

Chapter 4. The Medevac Mission

1. Author correspondence with Chief Warrant Officer David Sheppard, Army Black Hawk pilot, October 25, 1999.

2. Paul Watson and Paul Richter, "U.S. Marines Take Fire, Kill 1 in Kosovo Attack," *Los Angeles Times*, June 24, 1999, p. A1.

3. Sheppard, July 20, 1999.

4. Ibid.

5. Sikorsky Aircraft Corporation, "UH-60L Black Hawk," January 4, 2000, <http://www.sikorsky.com/programs/blackhawk/UH-60l.html> (April 27, 2000).

6. Derived from *Jane's Encyclopedia of Aviation* (New York: Portland House, 1989), p. 815.

Glossary

aerodynamics—The science that deals with the forces acting on an object when it moves through the air.

collective pitch control—Equipment in the helicopter used to fly the vehicle up and down.

cyclic pitch control—Equipment in the helicopter used to fly the vehicle forward, backward, and sideways.

downdraft—The strong down rush of air created beneath the rotor blades.

FAA—Federal Aviation Administration; oversees and regulates aircraft and pilots.

FLIR—Forward-looking infrared sensor. FLIR detects the heat from an aircraft's body and engine and displays it on a monitor similar to a television screen.

fuselage—The main body of an aircraft.

Global Positioning Satellite (GPS)—A system of satellites that gives exact location of an aircraft and other vehicles anywhere in the world.

heat signature—The white heat image from an aircraft on an infrared screen.

hover—To stay in the air without moving in any direction.

hydraulic systems—Systems such as power steering or braking that involve the use of a liquid, such as water, to increase force.

lift—The force created by the rotor blades that enables the helicopter to rise.

main rotor—The four large blades on top of the helicopter that rotate to lift the vehicle into the air.

Mayday—An emergency call from a ship or an airplane.

medevac—*Med*ical *evac*uation: flying a sick or injured person to a hospital.

preflight—A visual inspection of the helicopter done before every takeoff.

rescue hoist—A long steel cable that is used to lift people up to the helicopter.

rotor blades—The blades on top of the helicopter that whirl around to produce lift or on the tail of the helicopter to stabilize spin.

SAR—*S*earch *a*nd *r*escue; when the Coast Guard searches for and rescues people lost or adrift in the ocean or stranded in some other remote location.

Special Operations—Secret missions in enemy territory.

standby (or alert status)—The status of a helicopter when it is ready to fly on short notice.

tail rotor—A set of small blades on the tail of most helicopters that keeps the fuselage from spinning.

Further Reading

Books

Chant, Christopher. *Military Aircraft*. Broomhall, Pa.: Chelsea House Publishers, 1999.

————. *Helicopters*. New York: Marshall Cavendish, 1989.

Maynard, Christopher. *Aircraft*. Minneapolis: The Lerner Publishing Group, 1999.

Scarborough, Kate. *Helicopters*. Hauppauge, N.Y.: Barron's Educational Series, Inc., 1994.

Stille, Darlene R. *Helicopters*. Chicago: Children's Press, 1996.

Sullivan, George A. *Modern Combat Helicopters*. New York: Facts on File, 1993.

Video

Aaron, Bill. *All About Helicopters*. Bill Aaron Productions. Truckee, Calif., 1995.

Internet Addresses

NASA. *Off to a Flying Start*. "Introduction to Flight." December 27, 1998. <http://ltp.larc.nasa.gov/flyingstart/module1.html>.

Sikorsky Aircraft Corporation. n.d. <http://www.sikorsky.com/programs/index.html>.

Smithsonian National Air and Space Museum. © 2000. <http://www.nasm.edu>.

U.S. Army. *UH-60 Series Black Hawk Combat Assault Helicopter*. <http://www-rucker.army.mil/Ideafolder/h60/h60.htm>.

U.S. Army. *U.S. Army Helicopter Photos*. July 7, 2000. <http://www-acala1.ria.army.mil/lc/cs/csa/aaphoto.htm>.

Index

A
autopilot, 17

B
Black Hawk helicopter
  flight computer, 18, 19, 20, 23, 24
  fuel tanks, 17
  hydraulic systems, 17
  instruments and controls, 15, 17, 26–30
  military use, 13, 34–41
  missiles, 13, 17
  missions, 6, 13–15, 41
  models, 42
  power and speed, 7, 17
  specifications table, 25
Bosnia, 13
Bust Team, 9, 10, 12

C
Cessna Citationjet, 6, 7, 8, 12
Combat Surgical Hospital, 40
Creech, David, 27

D
Dustoff, 34, 35, 38

F
Firehawk, 42
flight medic, 36, 37, 38
flight plan, 17
flight simulator, 32

Fort Rucker, Alabama, 30
forward-looking infrared sensor (FLIR), 7, 9, 10, 12, 24, 31

G
Global Positioning Satellite (GPS), 23
Grenada, 19
gunship, 13

H
Haiti, 13

J
Jayhawk, 12, 20, 22, 23, 24, 30, 42

K
Karson, Larry, 6
Korean War, 39
Kosovo, 13

L
landing zone, 36, 37

M
Macedonia, 34
Mayday call, 22
McCullars, Jeffrey, 22, 23, 24, 28, 29
medevac, 33, 35, 36, 38, 39, 40, 41
Mobile Army Surgical Hospital (MASH), 40

N
National Aeronautics and Space Administration (NASA), 15
Nightsun, 9, 11,

night-vision goggles, 8, 30, 31, 32, 33

O
Operation Desert Storm, 20
Operation Urgent Fury, 19, 20

P
Pave Hawk, 14, 42
Persian Gulf War, 20
pilots, 6, 24, 26, 27, 35
  training, 29–33
preflight checklist, 36

R
Reagan, Ronald, 19
rescue swimmer, 29, 24
Riordan, Tim, 6–12
rotors, 8, 11, 12, 15, 26, 29, 37

S
Saudi Arabia, 20
Seahawk, 14, 42
search and rescue (SAR), 20, 22
Special Operations, 14, 20

U
U.S. Air Force, 14,
U.S. Army, 30
U.S. Coast Guard, 14, 20, 22, 24, 30
U.S. Customs, 5–6, 11, 12